The Great Fire of London

Written by Hawys Morgan

Illustrated by Ludovic Salle

Collins

It's one in the morning. A fire races up the walls of a bakery on Pudding Lane.

The baker and his family know they must take action.
They wrench open a window and escape over the rooftops.

Church bells disturb the peace — something is wrong!
People race along the streets, knocking loudly
on doors. They shout wildly. Fire is **menacing**
the city of London!

4

By six in the morning, the streets are full of confusion. Voices in **concerned** conversation say that three hundred houses burned down in the night. Now one hundred burn every hour!

river

London Bridge

Pudding Lane

Tower of London

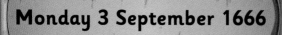

Monday 3 September 1666

Fire leaps across the narrow spaces between the houses.

It climbs the walls as hot **embers** fall, burning the people below. Half the city is destroyed.

The easterly wind forces the fire onwards. It has not rained since last month, so the dry wooden houses catch fire easily. The combination of dry weather, wooden houses and wind means the city is a **furnace**.

People quickly pack their possessions. They kneel in their gardens, hiding their treasures, like sugar, spices and expensive cheese, in pits.

sugar

Smoke circles people as they escape. They wrap fabric over their faces to protect themselves from the **toxic** smoke.

A huge **procession** of people clutch their possessions. Their only option is to leave the city.

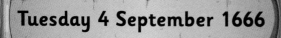
Tuesday 4 September 1666

Fire wrecks the shops in Cheapside, making the paint wrinkle on the shop signs.

The king gives instructions to destroy everything in the fire's path to slow it down. Families glance sadly back at the destruction of their homes.

The roads are so hot they burn people's feet.

At the riverside, there are hardly any boats left. People jump as the warehouses explode like bombs.

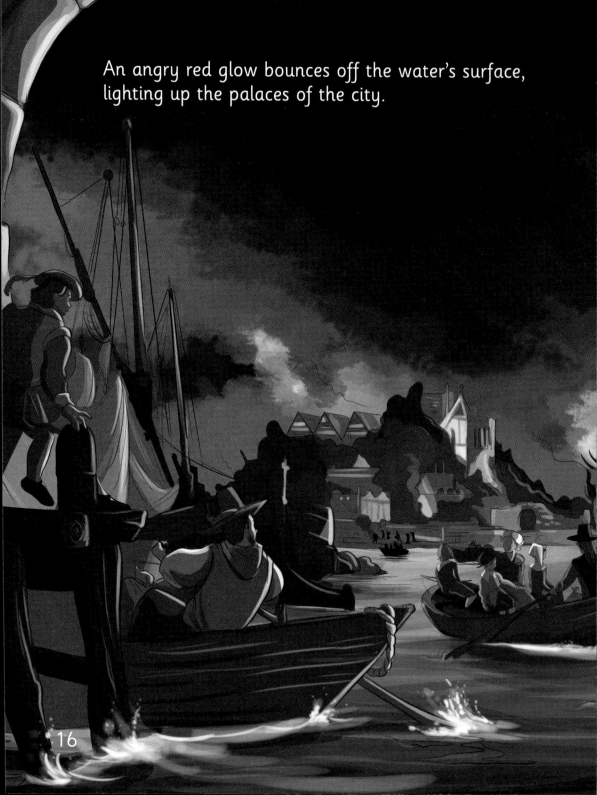

An angry red glow bounces off the water's surface, lighting up the palaces of the city.

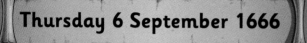

On land, men's muscles ache as they use axes, fire hooks and leather buckets to bravely fight the fire. Even the king and his brother are helping!

18

The fire is finally under control, but most of the city has been destroyed.

Tower of London

river

London Bridge

19

The king is concerned about the many homeless people. The price of bread is very high. He orders that bread is handed out.

Many thousands of houses have been destroyed.
Over the coming months there will be discussions
about an improved design for the city.
London will never be the same again.

Timeline

The fire starts in Pudding Lane. Hundreds of houses are burning every hour.

Half the city is destroyed.

Houses are destroyed to stop the fire.

Wednesday

Most fires are put out.

Thursday

Rubble is cleared and bread is given to the poor.

Glossary

concerned worried

embers small pieces of burning wood

furnace a large, hot oven

menacing threatening to harm

procession a group of people walking steadily forward

toxic bad for your health

After reading

Letters and Sounds: Phase 5-6

Word count: 499

Focus phonemes: /n/ kn, gn /m/ mb /r/ wr /s/ c, ce, sc /c/ x /sh/ ti, si, ssi, s

Common exception words: of, to, the, are, one, their, people, door, poor, great, water, any, improved, many, hour, half

Curriculum links: History

National Curriculum learning objectives: Reading/word reading: apply phonic knowledge and skills as the route to decode words; read accurately by blending sounds in unfamiliar words containing GPCs that have been taught; read other words of more than one syllable that contain taught GPCs; read aloud accurately books that are consistent with their developing phonic knowledge; re-read books to build up their fluency and confidence in word reading; Reading/comprehension: link what they have read or hear read to their own experiences; discuss word meanings; discuss the significance of the title and events

Developing fluency

- Take turns with your child to read a page. Model reading with fluency and expression.
- Look at the glossary. Can your child find these words in the main text? Practise reading the words in context.

Phonic practice

- Ask your child:
  - Look through the book. What words can you find with the /sh/ sound? (*action, conversation, combination, instructions, destruction*)
  - Can you identify the suffixes in these words: wildly, loudly, knocking, concerned, burned, quickly, menacing, destroyed, burning? (*wildly, loudly, knocking, concerned, burned, quickly, menacing, destroyed, burning*)

Extending vocabulary

- Ask your child:
  - The fire destroyed London. Can you think of any other words that mean **destroyed**? (e.g. *broken, ruined, damaged*)
  - What does the word **possessions** mean? (e.g. *belongings, things, stuff, property, valuables*)